THE MODERN RHYME

RITIKA DAWALIA

BookLeaf Publishing
India | USA | UK

Presentation by *BookLeaf Publishing*

Web: www.bookleafpub.com
E-mail: info@bookleafpub.com

ISBN: 9789367392850

First edition 2025

DEDICATION

To the magic of words, which hold the power to heal,
if you believe in them.

Contents

Preface

This book is a collection of verses about love, confusion, contemplation, growth and clarity woven into stories by the author.

Poetry is not simple even when the words are. At their best, these words only convey the immediate thoughts that one feels while going through the motions of life which are ever-changing.

However, some thoughts are captured as they are, when we sit with pen and paper in hand and just for a minute, the moment stops.

Acknowledgement

To my family and friends, who reminded me that my words matter and can be a catalyst for change in someone's life.

For every reader that picks up my book, I hope you find some comfort and courage in these pages.

To myself, for putting my thoughts into words when I needed to hear them the most.

Lastly, to the experiences that have inspired my poetry.

Yellow/of love

i. i warm my own heart

Months of distance from you
and in the aftermath of the war, from myself
showed me what cold was in the middle of summer
curtains closed for months
flowers didn't blossom
I stopped watering them
I stopped watering myself
I stopped everything when you left this
Distance seeped between my heart and mind
And anyone who tried to love me
My body was no longer mine
I was floating through life
But I was full of heaviness
Suddenly after months
I am now taking all the time for myself
I do not require this

I did not require you
I warm my own heart
I set it on fire
Every emotion for anyone who burnt me
No flowers for mourning what was
At the plant I dedicated to you
Whose twin dried and died because we did
No water seeped in
The roots were long dead
but I'm tending to the soil now
This mess of what is left
It will be winter soon
My warmth is eternal.

ii. different

I hope you do not become a clone
of all the people you surround yourself with
of the postings you see all day and night
of the music they play on the radio these days
I hope you can keep the light in your eyes
I hope you stay different
my sweet little son
my prettiest daughter
take life in good fun
I hope you do not become

like them grumpy ones
the ones who carry endless misery
I understand that multiple hurt
can make your heart of sand and stone
But for once, let the rain wash away
all the traces of pain
read new books
and write new pages
slowly but surely
the chapters of pain end
and life gives you a chance
to begin, yet again.

iii. i used to fall in love so easily

I used to fall in love so easily
With pretty eyes
Dark hair and a tall frame
Some right angles of limbs and I was in deep awe
And now I'm a little careful
I tread with caution
Are you good to me?
When you are upset at the world
What are you upset about?
Can you tell which smile is true from false
And what is wrong from right?
Do our core values even align?
Do you also like holding hands when we walk
With not a care in the world

Do you like taking long strolls in the dark?
With only the lights of the shops that surround us
Do you love going for long drives when it rains?
Are you ambitious about something which aligns and provides?
Have you healed? Are you trying?
Do you understand that
It matters
It is easy, when you want it
Be honest
What's the point if you don't feel it too?
Best leave now than later
I used to fall in love too easily
Now I know—
Patience is a virtue
You cannot learn all about a person in two weeks
Months and years pass by
You have to be willing
You don't want anything more when you love
Things happen
You make it happen.
You see possibilities.

iv. when memory fades

So when my memory starts to fade
I hope I still remember you.
Walking sunshine on the earth
dust yourself off of the past
the present is in your hands
and the future is your destiny
So, when memory fades, oh my sweet girl
I hope you still remember me.

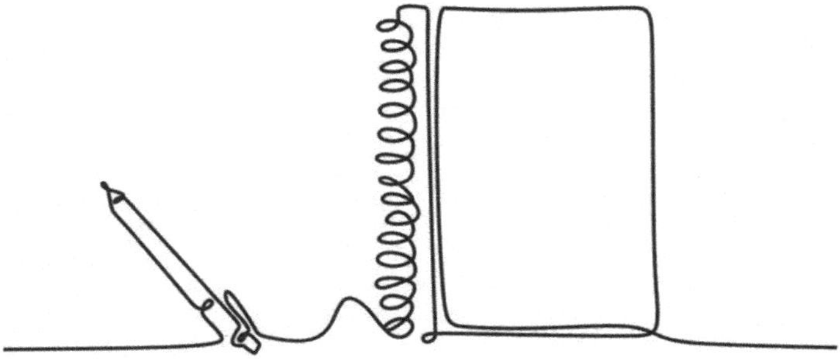

Purple/of confusion

v. a tale of two minds

My rational mind tells me
to get harsh with the world
but as soon as I behave the way they do
I break down, internally
something shatters and hurts me
more than it hurts them
I am love and want to be known for it
I do not give it away freely—
it is far too valuable
but I can sense when it is lacking
and when it is required
I believe we all must carry that compass within us
I am aware that we all don't
but my heart beats in sync with yours
And animal instincts can be silenced when you realize you are
not

just a push away from being a puppet of
wavering and ever-changing emotions
Take control
you are not clay now, no longer a child
They cannot mould you now
You do not have to shape-shift
emotions, hearts, and life are not things for you to play with now
a tale of two minds
think, breathe, think again
think right
there is no gray
breathe in, breathe out
let it go and then, begin.

vi. timeline

I had this timeline for me
which I had idealistically laid out for myself
where I had thought by this age I would have achieved this
and by that age, I will have achieved that
it's cute how I ignored that life is full of ups and downs
we are humans after all
we are all figuring it out as we go
we cannot be just folded, like paper
or be put in well-shaped moulds, to make a design
let yourself explore
of course you need to be stable
healthy and have some sense
and you want to be called wealthy
have faith, work hard
you will get there

sometimes even effortlessly
you will glide into
the life that is meant for you
the people will come
your nights will get easier
your mornings will be fun again
learn to trust again
not everyone is going to deceive you
people are people
they do mess up
some of them are truly messed up
sometimes even you'll mess up
it is not your part to fix them, but fix you
leave them, let them be
take care of your heart
sweet one
take care of yourself
do not force this timeline on yourself
sure it would have been nice in order
all proper
but then, there would have been less flexibility
right or wrong, you choose this life
some part of it
some part of you
embrace this journey
everything will be good
promise yourself you are going to make it good.

vii. ship wreck

What a hellish place to live in
a mind which has no peace
peace is not a stable guest
and guests are meant to leave
love enters and excites us
and when it leaves, I break and it all shambles
everything crumbles before my eyes
of sweet things that once used to be
I know I cannot forever let these feelings rule me
but I am entirely made up of what I feel
and if I feel nothing I feel like I cannot do anything
I am a ship wreck at this moment
I don't know how heavy is the weight I am carrying
of expectations I might or might not deliver
and I do not want to sink forever.
And I know it gets better

I will do better
I cannot always sit and think
I am going to move better
And now,
I might make a ship wreck, let things crumble this time
Better than becoming one.

viii. gas chamber

This isn't too extreme I hope
but there were days of such suffocation
I couldn't breathe with air all around me
no one was stopping me
and yet I felt so restricted
the walls were not there yet
the cage of being not valued
of being overlooked by some you put on a pedestal
and then you feel so much below
So, I don't want to know
what happened after I left.
I know I can breathe,
I just needed a breather
I now feel so free and light
so say what you want to say
shout it out loud
your truths and your lies
I am light as a feather.

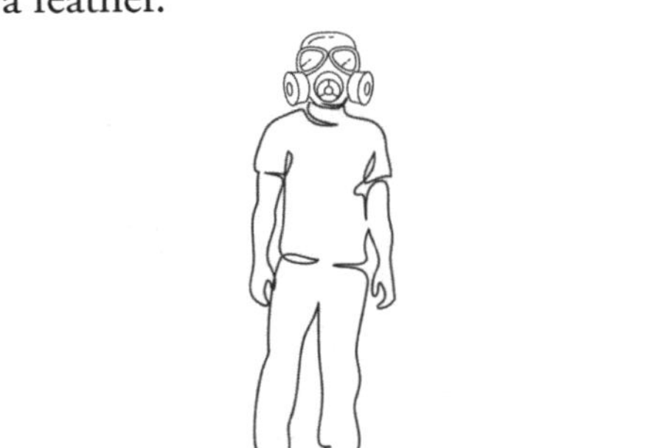

Blue/of contemplation

ix. dear new city

Dear New City,
you have housed me for over a week now
and I could not be more thankful
for what a great experience this has been
I was only a little nervous
when I was on my way here
packing whatever belongings I could
rolling them up and rushing to the airport
but after a day or two here
I slowly became accustomed to things
like the rain, the kitchen, the lights
the TV and the machine
and a couple of people
I found here through my family

I found a new space to be
I traveled to a local café
which spoke of pretty hummingbirds
had books behind the seats
and I picked one while feeding on chicken tenders
and a peach iced tea
and then I visited museums
and a gallery of art
I bought some bookmarks
and saw some art
and then the strangest and funniest thing of all happened
when I collided with someone
who I saw on the screen
and oh god, that was really strange but fun
As he was selling art
so the next couple days
I visited the monuments nearby
I had to convince some, that the local places
are as worthy as we are
and should not be ignored
as therein lies the true art and the true heart
We also went to a club
had a drink and some snacks
the music there was too loud
but my god, was it just the best
the bartenders were playing
with bottles that had their tops set on fire
an all-black dress code to shake it up
I truly believe that all of us girls,
just looked fire!

so bought some hanging birds with an egg in the nest
the next day quickly came and I decided to take some rest
in the late evening, we went to a small fest
where I bought two pair of sandals
a tie-up slipper in blue
and glittery blue flats
for when the occasion calls
I have three more days before I leave this city
I have a bookstore to visit
a cute one with two floors
and a fort that I've been told
that I must definitely go to!
So this is how it has been
in a place away from home
the food is stocked with old items
but there is an abundance of sorts
of mostly the unhealthy kind
but it is okay
because it has made me realize
the importance of choices
we make
of people or food or whatever
it all adds up and it all counts
the new city is nice, but I am still homebound.

x. and then they ask you to go

I will tell you a tale of this year's early months
a naive woman crossed paths with a guy with a dark embrace
and he pretended to listen and like he wanted to understand
what hid behind that face
so he embraced her each night with warm talks
of love and light
and showed her he was present
and she thought, *wow, what a present*
so they spent time together
saw movies, shared letters
he told her he likes to cook
and she told him, *oh wow*
I could have never guessed from your looks
sent her pictures of the sweets he cooked

and told her how his mother
never lets him cook
he has no father
just sister and his mom
and she hugged him in her mind
and now so long
he went to his native place
for a couple weeks
but before he left her for days
she gave him some tea leaves—
something organic, her sister brought home
and she wanted to share with him
something that felt like home
so she wrapped it with ribbons, of color red
their last good outing together
was a movie they watched in the night
and some bread
a sweet dish they shared with two spoons one cup
and then days passed with only a phone
that became a savior
she doesn't know what happened to him in the meantime
maybe it was her mother
maybe, just life
maybe the realization of things piling up
decided to pull back all warmth in the last couple days
and said, *whatever this is*
it has no space
and I simply cannot do it anymore
I want no kids, I want this no more
so she said, *are you sure?*

we have something good here
I do like this and would like to take it forward
he said he knows, and that is why it has to end
and she said *okay, adios then,* and that is the end.
But after she put that phone down
she gently sobbed between the four walls
called up her friend, a dear one at that
said, *I was almost falling in love*
and this man turned out to be the worst
the friend consoled the little swan
the poor lad, knows nothing about what he has lost
and time will tell who won or whose loss it was
but for now
I pray, you never find that woman again
and look for her everywhere.

xi. i do not think everyone self-reflects

It is a scary thing to do—
To accept that we have done wrong
or thought wrong about someone
or something along the same lines
and I do not think everyone has the strength to self-reflect
of course, it makes no one superior or inferior
but it does draw a line
and shows what kind of people we are after all
does it kill a part of you
that needs to go
and are you ready for the growing pains
of a new part of you that will emerge after you embrace your

mistakes
and promise to do better
not everyone can do this
but I struggle talking to people who cannot do it
they are just not capable of empathy
because they see it all
through a very tainted lens
a lens of jealousy
a strange kind of jealousy
of not being a better person and
hating those, who are.
I do not think everyone self reflects
it takes strength
and I do not think
Everyone has it.
They might break,
because it stops you for some time—
like brakes
Are you ready to own up?
Think.

Green/of growth

xii. earthless

Can we connect without suffocating each other
Can you hold my hand and love me clothed
Can I try to understand why you get dark thoughts
and can you handle my sunshine?
Can we plant trees on this land
Can you help bloom my garden
Do you think you can water the seeds you might sow
Can we build an orchid of beauty and growth together?
and there is no one to stop me
If it is you who I want to tend to
but you need to make it obvious you want to tend to the garden
appreciate the flowers
handle the soil mix, with insects and all.
It is summer still, but it is beginning to look
A lot like fall.

xiii. the trick is to live everyday

When the week has been rough
And you feel weak
and your shoulders start to round
and you can no longer stand tall
the trick is to give yourself some time
rest your tired eyes
then when you get up
look at one nice thing
listen to one nice word
read one nice paragraph
and take one deep breath
inhale, exhale it
out with the sadness you carry
see this day was served to you
on a platter more beautiful than gold

this is no secret to be told
you have it in your hand
make the best use of it
do not compare
do not hate
love yourself
do this for you
do this for those who will come after you
trust and work in the direction
take your mind off that thing that occupies it
and pays you no visit
the trick is to live everyday
like it is the best day
not once a year when you turn a year older
appreciate now
what are you doing
holding on to that frown?

xiv. a long time coming

This, what is finally happening in life
has been within me, aching to come out
whispering in my ear, asking me to speak out loud
to scream, to mention and display
that all this water is not quenching my thirst
that the flavor of life
is not in technicalities for me
not in being the one analyzing all day
that my soul blooms only in colors
like roses of different shades
but only in sunlight can I be myself
the night holds terrors and I like warm embraces
the harshness outside is nothing compared to how loud
I can roar, I can be
what I want
who I need to be
I am finally becoming
It was a long time coming.

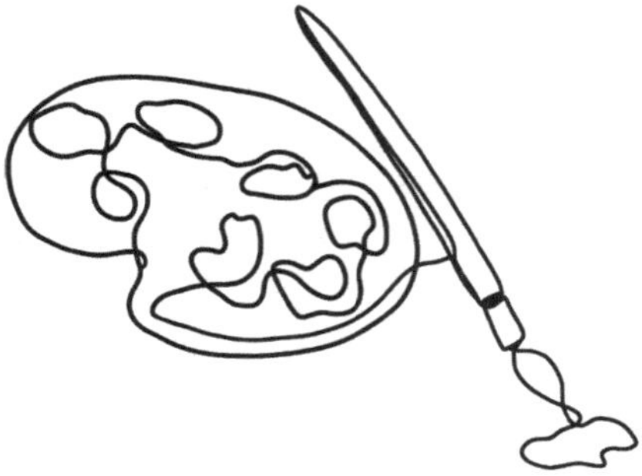

xv. come out of it

It is hard
I am not going to ignore these feelings
coming out of it once is hard enough
and again and again is just like torture
life is like this:
you learn or you repeat
I guess sometimes we have to do things we hate
to come out of it
If you see nothing else
and to come out of whatever it is
you have to do work you dislike, a job
you have to do it for you
and it has to get better for you
live, I have been dying to live.

xvi. release

You can only release the trauma
by reliving some of the worst times
wishing you had more courage
wishing you had someone to guide you
but it is okay, you have yourself now
you have learnt and you have grown
you have learned to navigate
through the darkest storms
but you do not have to be
everyone's favorite couch
you do not have to let
the ungrateful on your lap or lie down beside you
you need not give everyone a place to sleep
especially when they are the ones
who have only ever made you weep
you can do and must do only
what is best for you and yours
and release the loathsome people
whose existence you wish to remove from your past.

xvii. breathe

Loosen your shoulders,
you can relax, it has been a while now
and there is no more time to cry now
don't tighten your body
you can drop the toughened-up look now
it's okay to slow down now
be a little vulnerable, let someone new in
friends, lovers, and people who you are yet to meet
you can walk at your own pace
slow and steady wins the race
mindlessly wandering along won't do you much good
it will only hurt you more
to put yourself through things that you know you don't want
breathe, it will be okay
breathe out, you are safe
because you know
what you want, from what you don't
and that is enough, now and forever.

Orange/of clarity

xviii. leave the charm at the door

When you enter my territory
leave your charm at the door
this facade you create
of honey and glitter
What are you overcompensating for?
be still
learn to breathe
Is it not exhausting?
a little charm I am okay with
but what is this, you trying to sound and be superior
so much so that it creates a divide
and you voice your greatness
it takes away your power

your powerful effect would have been the flaws
the natural things you do not try to fix—
the smile
the giggles
the unstyled hair, the double texts
I see your scars, I see when you tug at your clothes
it is okay, are you okay?
What are you afraid of?
and that sense of accomplishment you get out of making
people feel insecure?
Does it contribute to the highs?
is your low so low
that you cannot even look yourself in the eye?

xix. a detached ambition

I am ruthless with the world
in soft ways
I just do not care
and yet I still play fair
I won't ever hit you on your wounds, ever
I will give you the time to lick them
heal and come
fight me if you must
look me in the eye
see the face of disgust
ashamed of your action
of how you deceived a friend in me
this second-hand embarrassment I have to carry on your behalf
the disgust of having been associated with your likes
who pretend that words and time matter

just to steal moments of sweet nothing
and from whom?
me? or yourself?
you can lie to me, yes
you can lie to your mother
but lying to yourself?
you must be really shallow and weak
inside, reading and speaking does not enlighten you
you just do not have the capacity to understand
you automate
and you are the machine.

xx. a thousand times over

A thousand twinkling stars covered the sky that night
I saw this in your beautiful deep black eyes
it was a cold winter evening and I was wearing dark green
we bought some books and your mother called
your eyes were twinkling so brightly I couldn't take mine off them
yet I looked down only for a second, to grab my cup in my hands
warming them up sip by sip, it's too warm, the conversations
I have had with you
were too strong,
the coffee is sweet
you always take the one that's black
and in me, that's something I lack
but I watch the time and the clock says we must leave

go to different places, there is too much to see
but I always wanted to travel the seas and the skies with you
I know you are doing all that
you always wanted to do
and trust me, I too am living my dreams
my eyes are wide awake
and in my sleep, I am in peace, in pieces
memories and flashbacks and movies
and music and life goes on.
yet, if you ask again—
for you, I would do it
a thousand times over and then again.

xxi. once a person turns cold

Once a person turns cold
and all the warmth has been soaked
and taken and taken
and never poured
you lose your hold
because once a person turns cold
you cannot make them understand
you can hold their hand
shake them, try to bring them back to life
revive what you killed in them, in yourself
but there is no safe place to land
because once a person turns cold
all the pages are fold
and kept on hold
if they loved you, if they told you
were you there to warm their frail frame when they looked at you
or did you look down

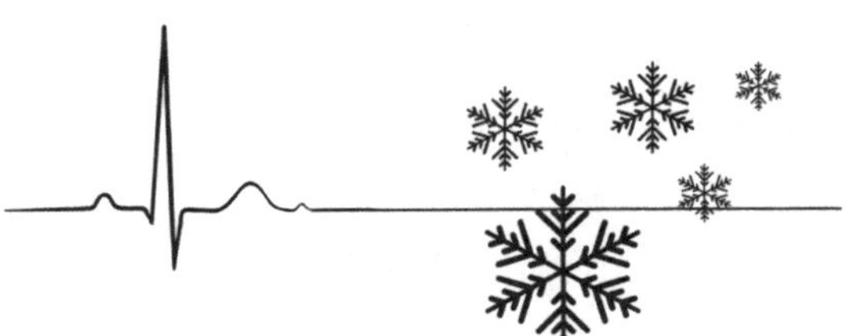

unable to meet their eyes
hiding the siren
the siren was loud
so loud,
and so many clouds
for so many days
the sun didn't shine
but once a person turns cold
there is nothing you do, that is worth a dime.
Save your time,
Save your life, it's alright.

Silver/of wisdom

xxii. moonshine

A few strands of gray have made their way to the crown
they add a mystic aura and an impeccable charm
I think they speak of the lessons learned
the long journey and the places we've burned
the paths we've crossed
and the roads we have blocked
the oceans we've swum
to the places we've landed
to the drinks we chugged
and mine is always tea
you know, the whims of the present
don't fancy me
the moonshine hair of your beautiful soul

the glimmers of hope in the darkness, urge me to stop and breathe
I've been too aware for too long
of so many things,
I haven't relaxed for a minute in a while
so for a while I'll stay here with you
and enjoy the moonshine.

xxiii. manifest and put effort still

When you find a stone
a shiny one
you are so intrigued by its beauty
then slowly, you get used to it
you think it is still special but you do not play with it
everyday
yet you do keep it near your eye
see it everyday, find happiness in knowing that it is yours
you let it comfort you
like a pillow between your arms
you hold it in the center of your palms
and feel the curves and no harshness
it's smooth
it is not a stone that cuts
it is not curated, just well-rounded

after years of work on self
you think you manifested it
you still have to put effort into knowing how to inculcate it in your life
if you lose the stone
you will realize it was a marble—
a marble you do not share
a marble you fear to lose
a marble so distinct in pattern
a marble only once you come across
not a stone
This is what is set in stone.

xxiv. i was there sitting across the table from you

I was there, was sitting across you from the table
I saw you were unsure
you were trying your best to make conversation
and I was leading it
I had this feeling a day before
I knew it was no one's fault
but I was never leading you on
you told me things which seemed genuine
and you frankly were not asking me for much
but you took my time
and my time is valuable
I spend it with intention
I value people and their time

experiences, memories
these are precious things
you do make it with many people
but who stays?
who do we keep?
do we all let go a little too easily?
are we taking people for granted?
did you think I will love everything and want to remember
these ruins?
never. I will forget you and each word you spoke
and you will never see me look at you the same way
this wasn't transactional
I deserved a better goodbye
if you had to leave like this.
there was no fight
there weren't arguments
we were up, talking each night
I see everything about you now
crystal clear
you are as false
and as good as one gets at the game—
like a true player.

xxv. i can still see it all

I can still see it all
and yet I minimize the tabs of our memories in my head
because remembering you, remembering us
hurts.
I can still see it all
the first time we talked
the feeling of being close to you
and I just can't wrap my head around the thought
that it was all in my head
because you left me
in each chance I gave you
because you just did not care about anything
I can see it all
so clearly now.
And I am okay with it,
Because I see it all
So clearly now.

xxvi. big black ocean eyes

If you had asked me to stay
I would have told you I love you
and how I have loved you ever since you left
but you didn't
you couldn't
I cannot stay when you do not ask me to stay
I cannot not look at you and pretend not to love you
keep your distance
I will keep living with this love
this one is mine
I do not have to share anything with you
I do not ask anything from you
Go then, if I am no reason to stay.
I have no reasons to pray
Not for this, not for you
For nothing at all, if this wasn't true.

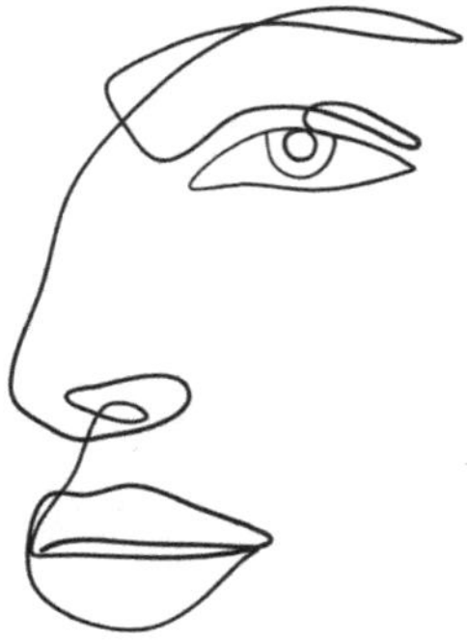

xxvii. uncomplicate the knots

It will rain and he will thunder
you will get upset, and you both will make blunders
but then the sun will rise again
and a rainbow will form
to the end of paradise
can you weather with me this storm?
It's not easy, to navigate these waves
when the wavelength is same but so different
but there are currents
and currently, I want to swim to the other side with you
I want to explore, the bright lights
the line that is the end of the sea
or the endlessness that is within me

I want to nurture a pearl and form
in a way an unshakeable bond
the pearl has its doors
your hand in mine
and mine in yours
you said you do not know if you want kids
because the world is truly in its maddest fits
and we are still learning the rights from the wrongs
but no one is perfect
and we do share a bond
I do not know about the future yet
but it is never fruitful to make the safest bet
we have knots below, just the surface
gift of ribbons around the beautiful wrapper
Is there something substantial between us
beneath the superficial chatter?
So let us uncomplicate the knots and see,
open and close the doors
of what you ask of me
to be true, I do not see
so far into the future
it is best we create each day as it comes
and see if this can lead us
somewhere where this can work.